World Book's Documenting History
African American Civil Rights Movement

WORLD
BOOK

a Scott Fetzer company
Chicago

www.worldbookonline.com

World Book, Inc.
233 N. Michigan Avenue
Chicago, IL 60601
U.S.A.

For information about other World Book publications, visit our website at **http://www.worldbookonline.com** or call **1-800-WORLDBK (967-5325)**.

For information about sales to schools and libraries, call **1-800-975-3250 (United States)**, or **1-800-837-5365 (Canada)**.

Library of Congress Cataloging-in-Publication Data

African American civil rights movement.
    p. cm. -- (World Book's documenting history)
  Includes bibliographical references and index.
  Summary: "A history of the African American civil rights movement, based on primary source documents and other historical artifacts. Features include period art works and photographs; excerpts from literary works, letters, speeches, broadcasts, and diaries; summary boxes; a timeline; maps; and a list of additional resources"-- Provided by publisher.
  ISBN 978-0-7166-1500-2
  1. African Americans--Civil rights--History--20th century--Juvenile literature. 2. African Americans--Civil rights--History--20th century --Sources--Juvenile literature. 3. Civil rights movements--United States--History--20th century--Juvenile literature. 4. Civil rights movements--United States--History--20th century--Sources--Juvenile literature. 5. United States--Race relations--Juvenile literature. 6. United States--Race relations--Sources--Juvenile literature. I. World Book, Inc.
  E185.61.A2385 2011
  323.1196'073--dc22
                                        2010017508

World Book's Documenting History
Set ISBN 978-0-7166-1498-2
Printed in Malaysia by TWP Sdn Bhd, JohorBahru
1st printing September 2010

Contents

What Are Civil Rights?

CIVIL RIGHTS ARE THE FREEDOMS AND RIGHTS that a person may have as a member of a community, state, or nation. Civil rights in the United States include freedom of speech, freedom of the press, and freedom of religion. Other U.S. civil rights include the right to own property and to receive fair and equal treatment from government. In democratic countries, a person's civil rights are often protected by law and custom (practices handed down from generation to generation). The constitutions of many democracies have bills of rights that describe basic liberties and freedoms.

1

2

We hold these truths to be *self-evident* [clear], that all men are created equal, that they are *endowed by their Creator* [given by God] with certain *unalienable Rights* [rights that cannot be taken away or given up], that among these are Life, Liberty and the pursuit of Happiness.

from the U.S. Declaration of Independence, 1776

▲ In a democracy, it is important that all citizens have the right to participate in government through their vote, no matter what their race or religion.

◀ The Declaration of Independence, the document by which the American Colonies declared their freedom from Great Britain, was adopted on July 4, 1776. The declaration established the *principle* (important rule) of civil rights—that all members of a society are *entitled to* (have the right to) the full protection of the law and the right to take part in government affairs.

3

1. Men are born and remain free and equal in rights. Social *distinctions* [differences] may be founded only upon the general good.

2. The aim of all political association is the preservation of the natural and *imprescriptible* [not able to be lost or taken away] rights of man. These rights are liberty, property, security, and resistance to *oppression* [cruel or unjust treatment].

3. The principle of all *sovereignty* [authority] resides essentially in the nation. No body nor individual may exercise any authority which does not proceed directly from the nation.

from the Declaration of the Rights of Man, 1789

◄ The Declaration of the Rights of Man was adopted by the French National Assembly on Aug. 26, 1789, during the French Revolution. The declaration sets forth the principles of freedom and equal rights.

▼ The famous lawyer Clarence Darrow (seated, center) defends Nathan F. Leopold, Jr. (left), and Richard A. Loeb (right). The two young men had admitted to police that they had kidnapped and murdered a 14-year-old boy in an attempt to commit the "perfect crime." Fair and equal treatment before the law guarantees that people arrested for a crime receive a trial and be represented by lawyers, even if they have confessed to the crime.

NOW YOU KNOW

- Civil rights protect the rights of individuals.

- Fair and equal treatment from government is an important civil right.

- In democratic countries, such civil rights as freedom of speech, freedom of the press, and freedom of religion are protected by law and custom.

Slavery

THE UNITED STATES WAS FOUNDED IN THE LATE 1700's on principles of freedom and equality, but these rights did not apply to women or black people. The rights granted to white women varied from state to state after the United States became a nation, but they never included most of the basic rights granted to white men. Worse still were the rights of slaves. Primarily people who had been brought to North America from Africa, slaves had no freedom or rights under U.S. law. They were considered the property of their owners.

▶ The U.S. Constitution, which created the nation's highest law, was written in 1787. The writers never actually used the word slaves. When they spoke of *slaves*, they called them "persons" bound or held "to service or labour." The Constitution declared that a slave remained a slave—that is, property—whether he or she was in a *slave state* (one that allowed slavery) or a *free state* (a state in which slavery was not permitted). Even if, for example, a slave escaped to a free state, that slave must be returned to his or her owner upon "claim of the party to whom such service or labour may be due."

1

No Person held to Service or Labour in one State [meaning slaves], under the Laws thereof, escaping into another, shall, in Consequence of any Law or Regulation therein, be discharged from such Service or Labour, but shall be delivered up on Claim of the Party to whom such Service or Labour may be due.

Article 4, Section 2 (3),
U.S. Constitution

2

They [slaves] had for more than a century before been regarded as beings of an inferior order and altogether unfit to associate with the white race, either in social or political relations; and so far inferior that they had no rights which the white man was bound to respect; and that the negro might justly and lawfully be reduced to slavery for his benefit. He was bought and sold, and treated as an ordinary article of merchandise and traffic, whenever a profit could be made by it.

Roger B. Taney, 1857

◀ In the 1857 *Dred Scott v. Sanford* Supreme Court case, Chief Justice Roger B. Taney (1777-1864) declared that no black person—whether free or slave—could claim U.S. citizenship; Congress could not prohibit slavery in U.S. territories; and finally, as private property, slaves could not be taken away from their owners without due process. This meant that slaves who had escaped into free states must by law be returned to their owners. The ruling moved the nation a step closer to civil war.

▶ an engraving of Dred Scott (1795-1858)

▼ By 1860, the United States had about 4 million slaves. The highest concentrations were in Virginia and North Carolina and across the "Deep South"—South Carolina, Georgia, Alabama, Mississippi, and Louisiana. In these states, slaves were used to work on plantations where tobacco, rice, *indigo* (a plant from which a blue dye was extracted), sugar cane, and cotton were grown in great quantities. Most of the crops were not processed in the South but shipped north or exported to the United Kingdom.

3 **Percent of slaves in total population by county**

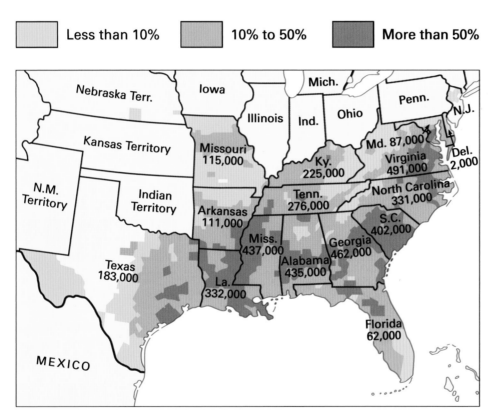

| Less than 10% | 10% to 50% | More than 50% |

NOW YOU KNOW

- The phrase "all men are created equal" from the Declaration of Independence originally referred only to white men.

- At the time the Constitution was written, women were not considered equal and could not vote.

- Slaves were regarded as property and, as such, had no rights.

Civil War and Emancipation

On Jan. 1, 1863, during the American Civil War (1861-1865), U.S. President Abraham Lincoln (1809-1865) issued the Emancipation Proclamation. This proclamation, or official announcement, declared that all slaves in the Southern states that were still fighting against the Union—the North and its armies—were freed. The Southern states in question were Alabama, Arkansas, Florida, Georgia, Louisiana, Mississippi, North Carolina, South Carolina, Texas, and Virginia. As Union armies fought across the Confederacy—the Southern states that left the United States at the outbreak of the Civil War—many slaves joined and fought with the Union. The 13th Amendment to the Constitution, which was *ratified* (approved) on Dec. 6, 1865, ended slavery in all parts of the United States.

1

◀ An 1888 facsimile of the Emancipation Proclamation bears an image of President Abraham Lincoln, the proclamation's author. The Emancipation Proclamation, which Lincoln issued on Jan. 1, 1863, declared slaves living in most of the Southern states to be free.

▼ In an editorial published in the *Douglas Monthly* in 1863, Frederick Douglass (1817-1895) urges men of color to join the Union Army. "Who would be free themselves must strike the blow" is a quote from British poet Lord Byron (1788-1824). Douglass and other *abolitionists* (people against slavery) strongly encouraged newly freed blacks to join the Union forces. By the end of the war, around 200,000 African Americans had volunteered.

2

"Who would be free, themselves must strike the blow." . . . I urge you to fly to arms and smite to death the power that would bury the government and your liberty in the same hopeless grave.

Frederick Douglass, 1863

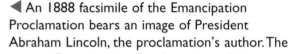

3

> Neither slavery nor involuntary *servitude* [forced labor], except as a punishment for crime whereof the party shall have been duly convicted, shall exist within the United States, or any place subject to their *jurisdiction* [authority].
>
> 13th Amendment to the U.S. Constitution, ratified Dec. 6, 1865

◀ The 13th Amendment granted freedom to slaves living anywhere in the United States and its territories. The only exception was forced labor for the punishment of a crime.

▼ A bronze bas-relief sculpture by Augustus Saint-Gaudens (1848-1907) honors the 54th Massachusetts Infantry regiment and its commander, Colonel Robert Gould Shaw (1837-1863), on horseback. The regiment was made up of free African American soldiers (except for the white officers). The 54th became famous on July 18, 1863, when more than 100 men, including the commander, died in an attack on Fort Wagner in South Carolina.

4

NOW YOU KNOW

- Slaves in Southern states fighting against the Union were emancipated in 1863.
- Many slaves joined the Union Army or Navy and fought in the war.
- The 13th Amendment to the Constitution, ratified on Dec. 6, 1865, ended slavery in the United States.

Reconstruction

RECONSTRUCTION (1865-1877) WAS A DIFFICULT PERIOD in the history of the United States following the Civil War. Political leaders of the North and South faced many complex questions during Reconstruction. How should the 11 Southern states that had *seceded* (withdrawn) from the Union be readmitted? How, if at all, should the Confederate leaders be punished? What rights should be granted to the approximately 4 million freed slaves? Congress eventually passed laws and proposed constitutional amendments to protect the rights of the former slaves and to give them the vote. The word Reconstruction also refers to the process by which the Union restored relations with the Confederate states after their defeat. Scholars still debate its successes and failures.

▲ An 1872 engraving of the first African Americans to serve in the U.S. Congress: (seated, from left to right) Senator Hiram Rhodes Revels of Mississippi (served 1870-1871); Representative Benjamin Sterling Turner of Alabama (1871-1873); Representative Josiah Thomas Walls of Florida (1871-1876); Representative Joseph Hayne Rainey of South Carolina (1870-1879); Representative Robert Eliot of South Carolina (1871-1874); and (standing, left) Representative Robert C. De Large of South Carolina (1871-1873) and (standing, right) Representative Jefferson Franklin Long of Georgia (1870-1871). During Reconstruction, Union soldiers stationed across the South protected the voting rights of black citizens, which were the majority in such states as Mississippi and South Carolina.

2

All persons born or *naturalized* [a legal process by which a person becomes a citizen of an adopted country] in the United States, and subject to the jurisdiction thereof, are citizens of the United States and of the State wherein they reside. No State shall make or enforce any law which shall abridge the privileges or *immunities* [freedoms] of citizens of the United States; nor shall any State deprive any person of life, liberty, or property, without *due process of law* [safeguards developed to assure that persons accused of wrongdoing will be treated fairly]; nor deny to any person within its jurisdiction the equal protection of the laws.

Section 1 of the 14th Amendment to the U.S. Constitution, ratified July 9, 1868

◀ The 14th Amendment to the U.S. Constitution granted citizenship to anyone born in the United States, including former slaves. Because former Confederate office holders and leaders were barred from holding office, and many Southern whites boycotted elections, African Americans were elected as representatives to state legislatures and the U.S. Congress during Reconstruction. This caused great resentment among whites in the South.

▶ In the versions of the poem "Respondez!" (Respond!) by Walt Whitman (1819-1892), which appeared in *Leaves of Grass* in 1871 and 1872, the American poet celebrates that the Civil War has turned the old order upside down; and he calls for a new order. During Reconstruction, radical members of Congress attempted to forge a new social order in the South, which was occupied by Union troops. This was deeply resented by many Southern whites.

3

(The war is completed—the price is paid—the title is settled beyond recall;)

Let every one answer! let those who sleep be waked! let none evade !

Must we still go on with our *affectations* (put on acts) and sneaking?

Let me bring this to a close—I *pronounce* (declare) openly for a new distribution of roles;

Let that which stood in front go behind! and let that which was behind advance to the front and speak;

Let murderers, *bigots* (prejudiced people), fools, unclean persons, offer new *propositions* (plans)!

Let the old propositions be postponed!

from "Respondez!" by Walt Whitman

NOW YOU KNOW

- The 12-year period following the Civil War is called Reconstruction.
- Congress passed constitutional amendments making former slaves citizens with the right to vote.
- Laws were also passed that prevented former Confederate officeholders from holding elective office.

Trouble in the South

NEWLY FORMED STATE GOVERNMENTS IN THE SOUTH began to rebuild their ruined economies. However, reconstructed state governments failed to win much support from Southern whites. Many Southern whites refused to accept African Americans as equals, and most African Americans continued to be poor and powerless. Some whites used violence to prevent African Americans from voting, terrorizing them into *submission* (accepting authority). Sharecropping, a system of farming in which a farmer works land for the owner in return for part of the crops, also kept African Americans in a state of near slavery.

1

◀ Most sharecroppers found themselves trapped in a web of debts to the landowner. The farm owner advanced credit to meet the living expenses of the cropper family until crops were sold. However, profits from crops rarely covered the debt, a system that generally kept sharecroppers as closely tied to the land as had the slavery that came before.

2

▶ In an article in *The Atlantic Monthly* magazine, Frederick Douglass, himself a former slave, worries that the South might slip back into conditions resembling slavery. He points out that the best way to protect the rights of blacks in the South is to ensure their right to vote.

Slavery, like all other great systems of wrong . . . has not neglected its own *conservation* [preservation] . . . Custom, manners, morals, religion, are all on its side everywhere in the South; and when you add the ignorance and *servility* [an attitude of a servant] of the ex-slave to the intelligence and accustomed authority of the master, you have the conditions, not out of which slavery will again grow, but under which it is impossible for the Federal government to wholly destroy it . . . The true way and the easiest way is to make our government entirely consistent with itself, and give to every loyal citizen the elective *franchise* [vote],—a right and power which will be ever present, and will form a wall of fire for his protection.

Frederick Douglass, December 1866

DOCUMENTING

3

We regard the Reconstruction Acts (so called) of Congress as usurpations [seizing a thing with force, but without the right], and unconstitutional, revolutionary, and void.

Democratic Party platform, 1868

◀ Opposition to Reconstruction policies in the 1868 Democratic Party platform reveals how divided the country was on the subject. Republican Party members were mostly in favor of it. Democrats, especially from the heavily Democratic South, generally opposed it. In the end, many Northerners lost interest in Reconstruction, partly because they were distracted by an economic depression that began in 1873, which produced social unrest and labor violence.

4

▶ An engraving from an 1874 issue of *Harper's Weekly* magazine depicts the Ku Klux Klan and the White League, two associations of white racists, joining hands to terrorize African Americans. The aim of both groups was to keep blacks from voting and asserting economic independence.

NOW YOU KNOW

• Sharecropping kept many blacks in a state of near slavery.

• Custom, manners, and lack of education all preserved the South's pre-Civil War social system.

• Such organizations as the Ku Klux Klan and the White League used terror to keep blacks from voting.

The Era of Jim Crow

DURING RECONSTRUCTION, MANY SOUTHERN WHITES could not accept the idea of former slaves voting and holding office, and they refused to take part in politics or elections in which black persons participated. After Reconstruction, however, whites gradually retook control of most Southern state governments. They passed laws to segregate the races, that is, to keep whites and nonwhites separate in public places. Laws were also passed to prevent African Americans from voting. Such measures, which became known as "Jim Crow" laws, held sway throughout the South and in some of the states that bordered the South by the early 1900's. The term "Jim Crow" came from a black character in a song from the 1830's.

▶ The Jim Crow laws enacted in Southern states enforced segregation, or the setting apart of the races, in almost every aspect of daily life. Southern states created ways to remove African Americans from *registration* (voting) lists. Some of these methods included *poll taxes* (taxes that had to be paid before a person was allowed to vote) and *literacy tests* (testing a person's ability to read). In fact, many African Americans could read, but *registrars* (officials who signed up voters) routinely excluded them anyway. So-called "grandfather clauses" in voting laws enabled whites who were *illiterate* (unable to read) to avoid the literacy requirement.

Jim Crow laws in

Alabama

The conductor of each passenger train is authorized and required to assign each passenger to the car or the division of the car . . . designated for the race to which such passenger belongs.

No person or corporation shall require any white female nurse to nurse in . . . hospitals, either public or private, in which negro men are placed.

Florida

The schools for white children and the schools for negro children shall be conducted separately.

Georgia

The officer in charge shall not bury, or allow to be buried, any colored persons upon ground set apart or used for the burial of white persons.

Louisiana

All circuses . . . shall provide . . . not less than two ticket offices with individual ticket sellers, and not less than two entrances to the said performance for each race.

2

> He [the voter] shall be able to read and write, and shall *demonstrate* [show] his ability to do so when he applies for registration. . . . No male person who was on January 1st, 1867, or at any date prior thereto, *entitled* [having the right] to vote under the Constitution or statutes of any State of the United States, wherein he then resided, and no son or grandson of any such person not less than twenty-one years of age at the date of the adoption of this Constitution . . . shall be denied the right to register and vote in this State by reason of his failure to possess the educational . . . qualifications prescribed by this Constitution. . . .
>
> Louisiana Constitution of 1898

◀ A grandfather clause is a law that excuses a person from a requirement because the person had a certain privilege or right at some time in the past. Grandfather clauses, such as this one in Louisiana, "grandfathered in" white voters who could not meet literacy requirements. The date of 1867 was chosen because it is before the passage of the 15th Amendment to the U.S. Constitution, which guaranteed voting rights to African Americans.

3

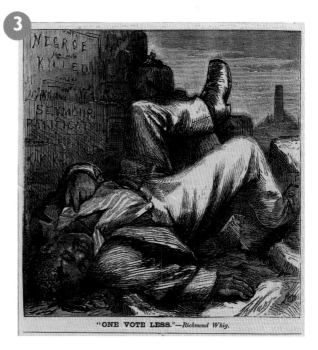

"ONE VOTE LESS."—*Richmond Whig.*

▶ A cartoon from a Richmond, Virginia, newspaper depicts a murdered black man above the caption "one vote less." The 14th Amendment, granting black men the right to vote, was ratified in July 1868. Many Southerners regarded every black man as a threat to the political power of white Southerners.

NOW YOU KNOW

- The term "Jim Crow" describes a set of laws designed to enforce separation of the races and to prevent African Americans from voting.
- Some states added "grandfather clauses" to their Jim Crow regulations to enable white voters to bypass the restrictions placed on black voters.
- Some whites used violence to enforce Jim Crow laws and keep segregationist governments in power.

Two African American Leaders

Around 1900, most African American leaders agreed that the living conditions of blacks, especially in the South, needed to be improved. However, the leaders did not all agree on how to achieve progress for African Americans. Two strong leaders emerged: Booker T. Washington (1856-1915) and W. E. B. Du Bois (1868-1963). Washington was principal of Tuskegee Institute, a vocational school—a school offering training for a business, profession, or trade—in Alabama. He urged blacks to stop demanding political power and social equality and instead to concentrate on education and jobs. Du Bois, a professor at Atlanta University, argued that Washington's acceptance of segregation would give whites justification to continue treating blacks unfairly because of their race.

1

▲ The Tuskegee Institute, which Booker T. Washington founded and led, followed the African American leader's social ideas. Students at Tuskegee concentrated on learning such practical trades as carpentry and agriculture.

▶ In a speech at the Atlanta Cotton States and International Exposition in 1895, Booker T. Washington states his belief that only jobs would bring progress to African Americans; political protest, according to him, was "extremist folly."

2

The wisest among my race understand that the agitation [disturbance] of questions of social equality is the extremist folly, and that progress in the enjoyment of all the privileges that will come to us must be the result of severe and constant struggle rather than of artificial forcing. No race that has anything to contribute to the markets of the world is long in any degree ostracized [sent away from the group or community]. . . . The opportunity to earn a dollar in a factory just now is worth infinitely more than the opportunity to spend a dollar in an opera House.

Booker T. Washington, 1895

◀ W. E. B. Du Bois urged African Americans to protest against Jim Crow laws. Du Bois founded the Niagara Movement to fight racial *discrimination* (treating one group differently than others). The movement led to the eventual formation of a major civil rights organization, the National Association for the Advancement of Colored People (NAACP).

▶ In "An Address to the Country" at the 1906 Niagara Movement Conference, W. E. B. Du Bois insists that the struggle for equal rights for African Americans is a struggle for the benefit of all Americans.

We will not be satisfied to take one jot or tittle [very small amounts] less than our full manhood rights. We claim for ourselves every single right that belongs to a freeborn American, political, civil and social; and until we get these rights we will never cease to protest and assail [attack] the ears of America. The battle we wage is not for ourselves alone but for all true Americans.

W. E. B. Du Bois, 1906

NOW YOU KNOW

- Not all black leaders of the early 1900's agreed on how African Americans should seek to better their lives.

- Booker T. Washington advised African Americans to work on bettering themselves through education and jobs and to wait patiently for full civil and political rights.

- W. E. B. Du Bois urged African Americans to join together in protesting against unjust Jim Crow laws and other forms of prejudice against blacks.

Conflict and Action

IN THE EARLY 1900'S, VIOLENT ACTS TOWARD AFRICAN AMERICANS erupted into race riots in several U.S. cities, including New York City in 1900, Atlanta in 1906, and Springfield, Illinois, in 1908. The Springfield riot prompted a group of prominent citizens to form the National Association for the Advancement of Colored People (NAACP) to fight against such violence and the racial discrimination that motivated it. Among the founders were W. E. B. Du Bois and other African American and white civic leaders and social reformers. Throughout the 1900's and beyond, the NAACP fought for racial equality through legal action, education, protests, and voter participation.

1

The best way to prevent a race riot depends entirely upon the cause. As to the present trouble in Atlanta, I would say that the only remedy is to remove the cause. So long as black brutes attempt assaults upon our white women, just so long will they be unceremoniously dealt with.

James G. Woodward, 1906

◀ Mayor James G. Woodward of Atlanta, quoted in *The Independent* on Sept. 27, 1906, blames African American actions for the Atlanta race riots. Scholars now state the attacks on white women reported by the mayor were untrue and were meant to influence an election that was taking place at the time.

▶ The Springfield race riot of 1908 as imagined by an illustrator for an Italian newspaper, *La Domenica del Corriere*. In August 1908, two African Americans accused of crimes against white women were being held in the county jail in Springfield, Illinois. An angry mob of whites gathered in front of the jail seeking revenge. The sheriff arranged to have the prisoners secretly moved to a nearby town. Learning of the sheriff's action, angry mob members went on a rampage, burning and killing in African American sections of town. In two days of rioting, they murdered two members of the African American community and destroyed dozens of black-owned businesses and houses.

2

3

If Mr. Lincoln could revisit this country . . . he would be disheartened and discouraged. . . . He would learn that the Supreme Court of the United States . . . had refused every opportunity to pass squarely upon this disfranchisement [loss of the right to vote] of millions, by laws avowedly discriminatory and openly enforced in such manner that the white men may vote and that black men be without a vote in their government . . . the spread of lawless attacks upon the negro, North, South and West—even in the Springfield made famous by Lincoln . . . could not but shock the author . . . [who wrote] "government of the people, by the people, for the people shall not perish from the earth." . . . Hence we call upon all the believers in democracy to join in a national conference for the discussion of present evils, the voicing of protests, and the renewal of the struggle for civil and political liberty.

The "Call," 1909

◀ A group of well-known American citizens, black and white, issued a "call" in January 1909 for a meeting on race relations to be held on the 100-year anniversary of Abraham Lincoln's birth, Feb. 12, 1909. The meeting, which actually took place in May 1909 in New York City, resulted in the founding of the NAACP, the National Association for the Advancement of Colored People.

4

▶ NAACP employees at the organization's national headquarters in New York City in 1933.

NOW YOU KNOW

- Racial conflict led to race riots in the North and the South in the early 1900's.
- Springfield, Illinois, the home of Abraham Lincoln, experienced a race riot in August 1908.
- A group of black and white civic leaders and social reformers founded the NAACP in 1909, in part to work against race-inspired violence.

The Campaign Against Lynching

MANY WHITES WERE AGAINST AFRICAN AMERICANS voting or holding office. Some resorted to violence and used threats, beatings, and "lynchings" to keep African Americans from exercising their rights. A lynching was the seizure and killing of a person, by hanging. It was used as much to terrorize the living as it was to punish the victim. The Tuskegee Institute recorded more than 3,400 lynchings of African Americans between 1882 and 1968. In 1915, the Ku Klux Klan (KKK)—a post-Civil War, anti-African American secret society—re-formed to terrorize African Americans and other minorities. Lynchings sometimes become public events, with hundreds of people attending them.

◄ A mob numbering in the hundreds watches Will James, a black man, being lynched in downtown Cairo, Illinois, on Nov. 11, 1909. Sharing in the culture of the South, many Cairo residents supported Jim Crow laws that kept the races segregated.

► At its headquarters, 69 Fifth Avenue, New York City, the NAACP flew a flag to report lynchings, until, in 1938, the threat of losing its lease forced the association to discontinue the practice.

◀ Ida B. Wells-Barnett (1862–1931)

▼ In "Lynch Law in America," published in *The Arena* in 1900, Wells-Barnett exposed the truth that the legal system throughout most of the South did not protect blacks; that an "unwritten law" allowed whites to murder blacks without *consequence* (a result or effect). In 1889, she became part-owner and a reporter for *Free Speech and Head-light,* a black-owned Memphis newspaper. After three of her friends were hanged in Memphis in 1892, she began to investigate lynchings of African Americans. Her work led to the founding of many antilynching organizations.

. . . It [lynching] represents the cool, calculating *deliberation* [plan] of intelligent people who openly *avow* [state] that there is an "unwritten law" that justifies them in putting human beings to death without complaint under oath, without trial by jury, without opportunity to make defense, and without right of appeal.

Ida B. Wells-Barnett, 1900

NOW YOU KNOW

- The KKK used lynching to keep African Americans from voting in elections and participating in public life in other ways.
- Thousands of African Americans were murdered by lynching between the 1880's and 1960's.
- Ida B. Wells-Barnett launched a national campaign against lynching.

The Great Migration

DISCRIMINATION AND BRUTALITY, COMBINED WITH POOR LIVING CONDITIONS, convinced many Southern blacks to move to the North during the late 1800's and early 1900's. During World War I (1914-1918) and into the 1920's, about 1 million Southern blacks moved to the North in search of a better life. Many of them were forced to live crowded together in cheap, unsanitary, run-down housing. After World War I, growing competition for jobs triggered increasingly *hostile* (angry and violent) race relations in the Northern cities. A series of riots erupted in the summer of 1919. At least 100 people died, and many more were injured.

▶ New York City-based writer and philosopher Alain Locke (1885-1954) described in his 1925 essay "Harlem" the mass migration of African Americans to Northern cities. Locke's reference to "medieval America" is his comment on the similarities of the feudal system of the Middle Ages and the sharecropping system that continued to exist in the South for much of the century following the American Civil War. Both economic systems tied people to the land, and both systems were maintained through fear and brutality.

1

With each successive wave of it, the movement of the Negro migrant becomes more and more like that of the European (white immigrants) waves at their *crests* [peaks], a mass movement toward the larger and the more democratic chance—in the Negro's case a deliberate flight not only from countryside to city, but from *medieval* [of the Middle Ages] America to modern.

Alain Locke, 1925

2

◀ An engraving from an 1879 issue of *Harper's Weekly* magazine depicts Florian Hall on the fairgrounds in Topeka, Kansas. The hall is filled with African Americans migrating west. In the late 1800's and early decades of the 1900's, African Americans in large numbers left the rural South for cities in the North and West. In 1870, the African American population in Kansas was approximately 16,000; by 1880, some 43,000 African Americans lived in Kansas.

3

Dear Sir:

I have been reading the Chicago defender and seeing so many advertisements about the work in the north I thought to write you concerning my condition. I am working hard in the south and can hardly earn a living. I have a wife and one child and can hardly feed them. I thought to write and ask you for some information concerning how to get a (railroad) pass for myself and family. I dont want to leave my family behind as I cant hardly make a living for them right here with them and I know they would fare hard if I would leave them. . . . Please dont publish my letter . . . we have to whisper this around among our selves because the white folks are angry now because the negroes are going north.

Lutcher, Louisiana
May 13, 1917

◀ In a letter to the editor of the *Chicago Defender* newspaper, an African American laborer from Mississippi asks for advice on how to move his family to the North to seek a better life. Although the black-owned *Chicago Defender* was based in the Midwest, the newspaper was widely distributed in the South, carried there by African American railroad employees.

4

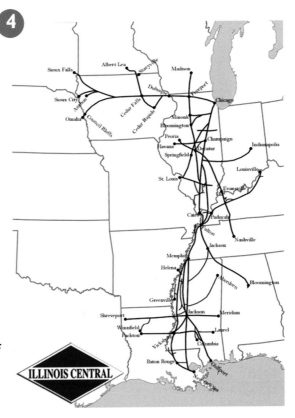

▶ The Illinois Central Railroad ran passenger routes between the lower Mississippi River Valley and the industrial cities in the North. Hundreds of thousands of African Americans took these routes to seek a better life in the North. Between 1916 and 1918, about 110,000 African Americans migrated to Chicago alone.

NOW YOU KNOW

- African Americans migrated in large numbers from the rural South to Northern industrial cities in the late 1800's and first decades of the 1900's.
- Many African Americans in the South learned about life in the North from black-edited newspapers carried South aboard trains.
- Competition between the growing number of blacks and nonblacks in Northern cities caused tension and led to race riots in some cities.

Black Labor and the New Deal

AFRICAN AMERICANS, LIKE MOST AMERICANS, STRUGGLED to survive the Great Depression—a worldwide economic slump of the 1930's. The Depression hit African American communities especially hard: racial discrimination gave a competitive edge to whites in a labor market with too few jobs; and many labor unions resisted admitting blacks. In 1933, President Franklin D. Roosevelt (1882-1945) launched the New Deal to pull the United States out of the Depression. The New Deal included programs of reform, relief, and recovery, and it benefited many blacks. However, discrimination continued even in government programs. A group of prominent African Americans, called the Black Cabinet, advised Roosevelt on the problems of African Americans.

◀ First Lady Eleanor Roosevelt (1884-1962), the wife of President Franklin D. Roosevelt (FDR), speaks at a 1939 National Conference on Negro Youth. Mrs. Roosevelt frequently carried concerns of the African American community to her husband. African American educator Mary McLeod Bethune (1875-1955) (left) was a prominent member of FDR's informal "Black Cabinet" and served as an administrator in the National Youth Administration, a New Deal relief program.

In recent years it has become increasingly the case where in many instances, the mother is the sole dependence of the home and, single-handed, fights the wolf from the door, while the father submits unwillingly to enforced idleness and unavoidable unemployment. Yet in myriads of [many, many] instances she controls home discipline with a tight rein and exerts a unifying influence that is the miracle of the century.

Mary McLeod Bethune, 1933

▶ In a June 1933 speech to the Chicago Women's Federation on "the progress of Negro women," Mary McLeod Bethune discusses the difficulties facing the African American family given the lack of jobs available during the Depression. She focuses on the importance of women to the unity of African American families.

▶ An African American porter helps passengers leave a Pullman sleeping car. Porters carried bags, turned down beds, and performed other jobs on special railroad cars made by the Pullman Palace Car Company of Chicago. In the first decades of the 1900's, the Pullman Company was the largest employer of African American men in the United States, with some 20,000 porters on the payroll. In 1935, under African American labor leader A. Philip Randolph (1889-1979), the Brotherhood of Sleeping Car Porters became the first African American union to join the American Federation of Labor (AFL).

The passing of slavery did not result in the complete emancipation of the Negro worker. As a matter of fact, the Civil War was not a complete revolution. It did not bring to the workers universal suffrage [the right to vote]. . . . More than any other groups in America, Negroes need to develop economic strength and organize with white workers to fight and abolish all forms and forces that attack their rights as workers.
A. Philip Randolph, 1935

◀ Speaking at the founding conference of the Negro Labor Committee in July 1935, A. Philip Randolph states that unions and organized labor held out the best hope for African American workers to be paid a fair wage.

NOW YOU KNOW

- The Great Depression of the 1930's was particularly hard for African Americans, who struggled with discrimination as well as economic hardship.

- Many African American workers tried to improve their economic situation by joining unions.

- President Franklin D. Roosevelt provided various forms of relief to Americans, including African Americans, but discrimination persisted even in government programs.

World War II and Its Aftermath

WORLD WAR II (1939-1945) OPENED UP NEW OPPORTUNITIES for African Americans in factories at which military equipment was made and in the armed forces. In 1941, at the urging of A. Philip Randolph (see page 25), President Franklin D. Roosevelt banned discrimination in defense plants by *executive* (presidential) order. However, troops served in segregated units throughout World War II.

1

Tout le Sang qui coule est rouge (All Blood Runs Red)

phrase painted on the plane of World War I ace Eugene Bullard

◄ "All blood runs red" is a reminder that all humans beings are alike under the skin. In World War I (1914-1918), Eugene Bullard (1894-1961), an African American, served as a combat pilot but not for the United States. When the war broke out, he was living in France, and he volunteered to fly combat missions for the French flying corps. His nickname was "the black swallow of death." When the United States entered the war in 1917, Bullard volunteered but was refused by the U.S. Air Corps because of his race. In 1994, long after his death, the secretary of the Air Force appointed him a second lieutenant in the U.S. Air Force.

2

▶ A black woman and a white woman work together in a defense plant during World War II. Because the war drained men from the work force, women were able to obtain high-paid factory jobs. After President Roosevelt ordered all factories with federal contracts integrated in 1941, defense plant managers were barred from segregating workers based upon race.

Keep us flying!

BUY WAR BONDS

◀ An image of a Tuskegee Airman—the pride of the African American community during World War II—illustrates a 1943 war-bond poster. In the early 1940's, the U.S. Army Air Corps remained segregated. No African American had ever served as a military pilot until 1941 when the Air Force started a pilot training school for African Americans at Tuskegee Institute, an African American university in Alabama. During the war, Tuskegee-trained pilots conducted combat missions. The program trained 996 pilots who served with great distinction, primarily in North Africa and Italy. On March 29, 2007, the surviving Tuskegee Airmen and the widows of deceased Airmen were awarded the Congressional Gold Medal at a Washington, D.C., ceremony in the Capitol Rotunda.

> It is hereby declared to be the policy of the President that there shall be equality of treatment and opportunity for all persons in the armed services without regard to race, color, religion, or national origin.
>
> President Harry S. Truman, 1948
> Executive Order 9981

▶ With a stroke of the pen in July 1948, President Harry S. Truman (1884-1972) desegregated the armed forces of the United States. The opening of the armed services to all Americans on the basis of merit struck at the heart of Jim Crow traditions.

NOW YOU KNOW

- In 1941, President Franklin D. Roosevelt issued an executive order banning racial discrimination in defense industries.
- On the fighting front, military units remained segregated throughout the war. The Tuskegee Airmen, a group of African American air force pilots, served with distinction.
- In 1948, President Harry S. Truman issued an executive order ending segregation in the armed forces.

Struggle for Quality Education

IN THE 1896 U.S. SUPREME COURT CASE PLESSY V. FERGUSON, THE COURT RULED that the 14th Amendment did not guarantee social equality, and it declared that providing separate school facilities for blacks and whites was constitutional. In 1954, a case—*Brown v. Board of Education of Topeka*—came before the Supreme Court that challenged segregated school systems. The NAACP's chief lawyer on the case, Thurgood Marshall (1908-1993), argued that schools separated by race could never be equal. In its unanimous ruling, the court declared school segregation by race illegal, overturning *Plessy v. Ferguson*.

▲ Black children attend an overcrowded school in Arkansas in 1949. Under segregation, African American schools typically were not as good as those for white students. They often lacked adequate equipment, and schoolbooks were often old editions discarded by the schools for white students.

▶ In 1955, *Time* magazine honored Thurgood Marshall with a cover story. In 1954, Marshall had argued against segregated schools before the U.S. Supreme Court in the case of *Brown v. Board of Education of Topeka* and won. Later, he served as the first African American justice on the Supreme Court of the United States (see also pages 42-43).

3

We conclude that in the field of public education the *doctrine* [idea] of "separate but equal" has no place. Separate educational facilities are *inherently* [by their very nature] unequal. Therefore, we hold that the plaintiffs and others similarly situated for whom the actions have been brought are, by reason of the segregation complained of, deprived of the equal protection of the laws guaranteed by the Fourteenth Amendment.

from the 1954 U.S. Supreme Court decision
Brown v. Board of Education of Topeka

◀ In *Brown v. Board of Education of Topeka*, Oliver Brown, an African American who lived in Topeka, Kansas, sued the local board of education for not allowing his daughter to attend an all-white school near her home. In a *unanimous decision* (all the justices in agreement), the U.S. Supreme Court concluded that separate schools could never be equal. Therefore, segregated schools violated the 14th Amendment, which requires that all citizens be treated equally.

▶ On Sept. 4, 1957, an angry crowd hurls insults at Elizabeth Eckford, one of nine African American students who tried to enroll in the then all-white Little Rock Central High School. The attempt by the "Little Rock Nine" to integrate the school was the first and most dramatic test of the Supreme Court's *Brown v. Board of Education of Topeka*. The governor of Arkansas, Orval Faubus (1910-1984), ordered state troops to block their entry. Finally, President Dwight D. Eisenhower (1890-1969) sent federal troops to Little Rock to escort the "Little Rock Nine" into the school.

4

NOW YOU KNOW

- "Separate but equal" was a doctrine of separation of the races that the U.S. Supreme Court approved in 1896. However, "separate" was rarely "equal."

- In 1954, the Supreme Court rejected the "separate but equal" doctrine in *Brown v. Board of Education of Topeka*.

- In September 1957, President Dwight D. Eisenhower sent federal troops to Little Rock, Arkansas, to force the integration of the city's all-white Central High School.

The Montgomery Bus Boycott

BEFORE 1956, PUBLIC TRANSPORTATION SYSTEMS IN THE SOUTH, such as buses and trains, were completely segregated. On buses, African Americans were required to move to the rear of the bus, where a small number of seats were reserved for them. In December 1955, Rosa Parks (1913-2005), an African American woman, refused to give up her seat to a white passenger on a city bus in Montgomery, Alabama. She was arrested. As a result of this arrest, blacks in Montgomery launched a *boycott* (an organized refusal to buy or take part in something) of the public bus system.

COLORED
WAITING ROOM
PRIVATE PROPERTY
NO PARKING
Driving through or Turning Around

BINGO
TONITE!

Good
Housekeeping

True Story
HITLER'S
LOVE LIFE
REVEALED

CH COMPANY

▲ The Durham, North Carolina, bus station, like all bus and train stations in the southern United States, had separate waiting rooms for black and white passengers in the 1940's. Before late 1956, all public transportation in the South was segregated.

▶ Rosa Parks writes in *Rosa Parks: My Story* that she refused to give up her seat because she was tired of being treated as a second-class citizen. She also recalled about that day: "I didn't want to pay my fare and then go around the back door, because many times, even if you did that, you might not get on the bus at all. They'd probably shut the door, drive off, and leave you standing there."

People always say that I didn't give up my seat because I was tired, but that isn't true. I was not tired physically, or no more tired than I usually was at the end of a working day. I was not old, although some people have an image of me as being old then. I was forty-two. No, the only tired I was, was tired of giving in.

Rosa Parks

▶ A police officer takes Rosa Parks's fingerprints in Montgomery on Dec. 1, 1955. She was arrested for violating a city law requiring that whites and blacks sit in separate sections on buses. The front rows were for whites only. The law required blacks to leave their seats in the middle rows when all seats in the front rows were taken and other whites still wanted seats. She refused to give up her seat when a white man asked her to move to the rear. Her act of *civil disobedience* (the deliberate and public refusal to obey a law) triggered a boycott of the bus system.

At the time I was arrested I had no idea it would turn into this. It was just a day like any other day. The only thing that made it significant was that the masses of the people joined in.

Rosa Parks

◀ The boycott that Rosa Parks spurred went on for more than a year. From Dec. 5, 1955, to Dec. 20, 1956, thousands of blacks, many of them completely dependent on the city's public transportation system, refused to ride Montgomery's buses. The NAACP built a case around the boycott, which it took to the U.S. Supreme Court. In *Browder v. Gayle*, the Supreme Court declared that segregated seating on the city's buses—and by extension, on all public transportation—was unconstitutional. The boycott's success encouraged other mass protests demanding civil rights for blacks.

NOW YOU KNOW

- Public transportation was segregated in the southern United States until late 1956.
- Rosa Parks defied bus segregation in Montgomery, Alabama, in 1955 and was arrested.
- NAACP lawyers took the case that grew out of Rosa Parks's arrest to the Supreme Court, which ruled that segregated seating on public transportation was unconstitutional.

A New Leader Emerges

DURING THE MONTGOMERY BUS BOYCOTT, MARTIN LUTHER KING, JR., emerged as the leader of the civil rights movement in the United States. King, who was well educated and a thinker, was a highly gifted public speaker. He had studied and admired the work of Mohandas Gandhi (1869-1948), who using civil disobedience and nonviolent tactics, had led India to independence from the United Kingdom in 1947. King applied the same tactics to the civil rights movement in the United States.

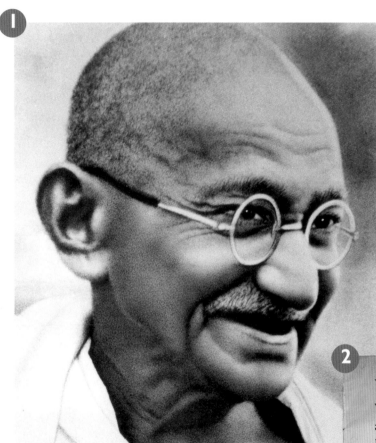

◀ As a young man, Mohandas Gandhi—called the "Mahatma," or "great soul"—developed a method of direct social action, based upon principles of courage, nonviolence, and truth, which he called *Satyagraha.* Under this system, the way people behave forces a change in the behavior of their oppressors. Meeting violence with nonviolence places the oppressor in a difficult, indefensible position. Gandhi used Satyagraha to fight for India's independence and to force social change.

▶ In his essay "My Faith in Nonviolence," Mohandas Gandhi preaches the strength of love over destruction. The Indian leader devoted himself to nonviolence and tolerance. India, however, was split by religious differences. On Jan. 30, 1948, just months after India gained its independence, a Hindu who opposed Gandhi's program of tolerance for all religions assassinated him.

Wherever there are *jars* [conflicts], wherever you are confronted with an opponent, conquer him with love. In a crude manner I have worked it out in my life. That does not mean that all my difficulties are solved. I have found, however, that this law of love has answered as the law of destruction has never done.

Mohandas Gandhi, 1933

▲ Martin Luther King, Jr., outlines the Montgomery bus boycott strategy to his advisers and organizers, including Ralph Abernathy and Rosa Parks (front row, left and center). King applied Gandhi's principles of nonviolence and civil disobedience to the African American civil rights movement.

▶ In his Nobel Peace Prize acceptance speech on Dec. 10, 1964, King acknowledged the influence of Gandhi's nonviolent movement for Indian independence on the U.S. civil rights movement.

After contemplation, I conclude that this award [the Nobel Peace Prize] which I receive on behalf of that movement is a profound recognition that nonviolence is the answer to the crucial political and moral question of our time—the need for man to overcome oppression and violence without resorting to violence and oppression.

Martin Luther King, Jr., 1964

NOW YOU KNOW

- Martin Luther King, Jr., became the leader of the civil rights movement in the United States after leading the Montgomery bus boycott in 1955.

- King was heavily influenced by Mohandas Gandhi, whose movement to free India from British rule was based upon nonviolence.

- Martin Luther King, Jr., was awarded the Nobel Peace Prize in 1964 for his civil rights work.

The Tactics of Nonviolence

IN 1957, MARTIN LUTHER KING, JR., AND OTHER AFRICAN AMERICAN LEADERS in the South founded the Southern Christian Leadership Conference (SCLC). The SCLC, with King as its leader, coordinated nonviolent civil rights actions for several years during the civil rights movement. Other civil rights groups, including the Student Nonviolent Coordinating Committee (SNCC, pronounced "snick") and the Congress for Racial Equality (CORE), also sponsored civil rights actions. These included sit-ins, Freedom Rides, boycotts, and marches. But nonviolence did not mean that no violence occurred; in some cases, nonviolent demonstrators were attacked by whites, or people not actually aligned with demonstrators joined in with violent results.

▼ Writing for the *Greensboro Daily News* in 1970, 10 years after the Greensboro sit-ins, staff writer Joe Knox notes the lesson that civil rights leaders took from the successful Greensboro sit-ins: No one was going to grant them their rights freely; they would have to take their rights by their own *initiative* (the readiness and ability to start something).

▲ College students in Greensboro, North Carolina, stage a sit-in at a local lunch counter in 1960. In a sit-in, people entered a place or business that discriminated and sat down. They refused to get up until their demands were met or until police arrested them. The demonstrators did not *resist* (fight) arrest. By allowing themselves to be arrested, demonstrators gained valuable press coverage to publicize their cause. The Greensboro sit-in resulted in the integration of the city's downtown restaurants later in the year.

Greensboro's first round of demonstrations aimed at lowering racial barriers in places catering to the public began with the lunch counter sit-ins at Woolworth's and Kress's variety stores in February 1960. They came to an end . . . when management of both stores went against "local custom" and made their food services available to all races. . . . But Negro leaders and young apprentices beginning to spearhead civil rights movements had to re-learn . . . an old lesson: Nobody was going to give them anything; if a door was to be opened it would have to be forced open.

Joe Knox, 1970

► In 1961, U.S. Attorney General Robert F. Kennedy (1925-1968) tried to persuade the head of CORE, James Farmer (1920-1999), to temporarily suspend his organization's activities, to give Southern segregationists "cooling off" time. Farmer's reply—"We have been cooling off for 350 years"—speaks of the lengthy wait for their rights that African Americans had endured. James Farmer had staged a series of Freedom Rides—*interstate* (between states) bus rides by black and white volunteers—into segregated Southern states. In 1960, the Supreme Court had ruled that segregation on interstate transportation was unconstitutional. Nevertheless, passengers continued to be segregated on interstate buses. Defying this custom, Freedom Riders faced extreme violence.

We have been cooling off for 350 years.
James Farmer, 1961

▼ A bus burns alongside a road outside Anniston, Alabama, in May 1961. The bus, carrying CORE's Freedom Riders, was attacked by a white mob and set on fire. The Freedom Riders escaped the burning bus, but many were badly beaten as they tried to flee to safety.

NOW YOU KNOW

- Martin Luther King, Jr., and other African American civil rights leaders of the 1950's and 1960's were committed to principles of nonviolence in their campaign against discrimination.

- Black students and others challenged segregation in restaurants by conducting sit-ins.

- African American and white volunteers participated in Freedom Rides to challenge the legality of segregation on buses that traveled between states.

Birmingham, 1963

IN EARLY 1963, FRED SHUTTLESWORTH (1922-), AN AFRICAN AMERICAN LEADER in Birmingham, Alabama, invited Martin Luther King, Jr., and other Southern Christian Leadership Conference (SCLC) members to take part in a nonviolent civil rights campaign against segregation policies in Birmingham, one of the most racially divided cities in the South. To control demonstrations, Birmingham's police chief, Eugene "Bull" Connor (1897-1973), obtained an *injunction* (order) barring the protests, and he raised the bail bond needed to get out of jail from $300 to $1,200. He later ordered police to turn fire hoses and dogs on peaceful protesters, many of them students. The Birmingham campaign proved to be a turning point in the civil rights movement.

▶ A police officer arrests Martin Luther King, Jr., (far right) and Ralph Abernathy (center) in Birmingham on April 12, 1963, on charges of violating the city's antiprotest injunction. Abernathy was an SCLC founder and a strong supporter of King. They were arrested with about 50 others on Good Friday. King was held in the Birmingham jail and was denied consultation with an NAACP attorney without guards present. King's supporters showered President John F. Kennedy with telegrams protesting the arrest.

▶ While in jail, King wrote "Letter from a Birmingham Jail" in response to criticisms by white religious leaders that he and other African American leaders were triggering violence by their demands for civil rights. The letter has become a classic of protest literature, justifying civil disobedience by people who are victims of discrimination and unfair laws.

Actually, we who engage in nonviolent direct action are not the creators of [racial] tension. We merely bring to the surface the hidden tension that is already alive. We bring it out in the open, where it can be seen and dealt with.

Martin Luther King, Jr., 1963

▶ Birmingham police use dogs on an African American teenager on May 3, 1963. Young people had been included in the protest because it would be less of a financial hardship on their families if they, rather than their working parents, were jailed. In homes across the nation that night, shocked Americans watched the violent acts against peaceful young protesters on the television news.

The events in Birmingham . . . have so increased the cries for equality that no city or state or legislative body can prudently choose to ignore them.

President John F. Kennedy,
June 11, 1963

◀ In 1963, President Kennedy recognized that television images of police attacking peaceful protesters in Birmingham had affected public opinion in the United States. Kennedy used the opportunity provided by the changing mood of the people to underline his support for equality and civil rights.

NOW YOU KNOW

- Birmingham, Alabama, was a strictly segregated city in 1963.
- African American leader Fred Shuttlesworth invited SCLC leaders to participate in a civil rights campaign in Birmingham in early 1963.
- In May 1963, Birmingham's police chief, Bull Connor, ordered violent police action against peaceful protesters. The shocking scenes on television persuaded many Americans to support the civil rights movement.

The Victims

ALTHOUGH MANY SOUTHERN WHITES REJECTED VIOLENCE, segregationists in positions of power—governors, prosecutors, mayors, and police chiefs—were determined to preserve segregation. In many areas of the South, the Ku Klux Klan (KKK) was active and willing to use violence to enforce separation of the races. Many of those carrying out the violence for the KKK were never brought to justice—or they were arrested and tried decades later.

▶ At approximately 10:20 a.m. on Sept. 15, 1963, a bomb exploded outside the basement of the 16th Street Baptist Church in Birmingham, Alabama. The force of the blast was so great it blew a hole in the back wall of the church. An 11-year-old, Denise McNair, and three 14-year-olds, Addie Mae Collins, Carole Robertson, and Cynthia Wesley, attending Sunday-school classes in the church basement, were killed. Fourteen years later, in 1977, Robert Chambliss was convicted for his involvement in the bombing. Thomas Blanton, Jr., and Bobby Cherry, in 2001 and 2002, respectively, were finally convicted for their participation in the murders. All were members of the Ku Klux Klan.

1

Birmingham, Ala., Sept. 15—A bomb severely damaged a Negro church today during Sunday school services, killing four Negro girls and setting off racial rioting and other violence in which two Negro boys were shot to death. . . . The bombing, the fourth such incident in less than a month, resulted in heavy damage to the church, to a two-story office building across the street and to a home. . . . None of the 50 bombings of Negro property here [in Birmingham] since World War II have been solved.

The New York Times, Sept. 16, 1963

2

The bodies of three civil rights workers missing for six weeks have been found buried in a partially constructed dam near Philadelphia, Mississippi. Agents from the Federal Bureau of Investigation found the three young men—two white and one black man—about six miles from the town in a wooded area near where they were last seen on the night of June 21. They were Michael Schwerner, aged 24, Andrew Goodman, 20, both from New York and James Chaney, 22, from Meridian, Mississippi. All were members of the Congress of Racial Equality (CORE) dedicated to nonviolent direct action against racial discrimination.

BBC News, Aug. 4, 1964

◀ The deputy sheriff who arrested the civil rights workers, Cecil Price, was a member of the KKK. Late on June 21, 1964, he drove them from the jail to a site where other KKK members were waiting to murder them. Price and 18 others were arrested in 1967, but Mississippi prosecutors were not willing to charge them with murder. Federal prosecutors subsequently tried the men for civil rights violations. Price and six others were found guilty and got 3 to 10 years in prison. One more defendant, Edgar Killen, a KKK organizer, was found guilty of three counts of manslaughter on June 21, 2005—the 41st anniversary of the crime—and went to prison at age 80.

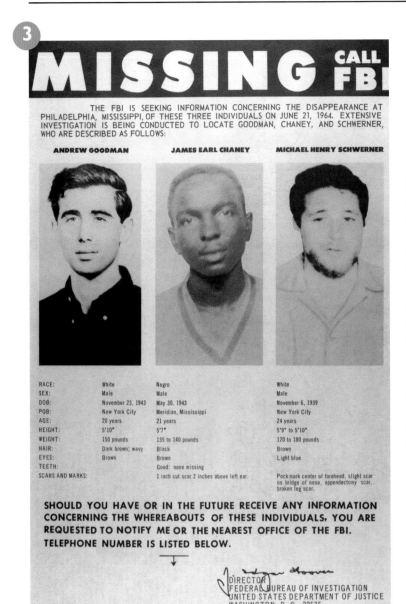

◀ A 1964 Federal Bureau of Investigation (FBI) missing persons poster shows photos (from left to right) of Andrew Goodman (1943-1964), James Chaney (1943-1964), and Michael Schwerner (1939-1964). Volunteers for the CORE (Congress on Racial Equality) "Freedom Summer (voter registration) Campaign," the three men were stopped by a deputy sheriff outside Philadelphia, Mississippi, on June 21, 1964, supposedly for speeding. When they failed to show up at CORE headquarters in Meridian, Mississippi, U.S. Attorney General Robert Kennedy was notified. He ordered the FBI to investigate.

NOW YOU KNOW

- Some Southern officials and white extremists were determined to preserve segregation.
- The Southern system of segregation was brutally enforced, often by members of the KKK.
- At the height of the civil rights movement in the 1960's, white prosecutors in the South were often unwilling to indict whites on charges of violence against blacks.

The March on Washington

As trouble brewed in Birmingham and other Southern cities, leaders of the civil rights movement, headed by A. Philip Randolph, planned a march on Washington, D.C., "for jobs and freedom" to take place in August 1963. In June, President Kennedy submitted legislation for a new civil rights bill to Congress, but few politicians believed that Congress would pass it. The organizers of the march wanted to send a signal to members of Congress that the public supported the civil rights legislation. Between 200,000 and 250,000 people, both black and white, came from all over the United States to participate in the march.

▶ Martin Luther King, Jr., stands before a crowd from 200,000 to 250,000 people on the National Mall, in Washington, D.C., during the 1963 March on Washington. King set the urgent but hopeful tone of the march with his "I Have a Dream" speech. King organized the event with labor leader A. Philip Randolph; executive director of the NAACP Roy Wilkins (1901-1981); civil rights activist Bayard Rustin (1912?-1987); and cofounder of CORE James Farmer. Farmer was unable to attend the march because he was in jail in Louisiana for organizing protests there.

2

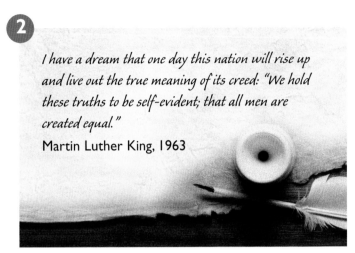

I have a dream that one day this nation will rise up and live out the true meaning of its creed: "We hold these truths to be self-evident; that all men are created equal."

Martin Luther King, 1963

◄ Martin Luther King, Jr., delivered his "I Have a Dream" speech on the steps of the Lincoln Memorial on Aug. 28, 1963. The speech would become one of the most famous addresses in U.S. history.

► At the March on Washington, John Lewis (1940-   ) spoke as the representative of the Student Nonviolent Coordinating Committee (SNCC). The speech Lewis had written was originally more controversial. In it, he stated that Kennedy's civil rights bill was "too little, too late." Civil rights leaders convinced Lewis to tone down the speech, but it was still the most controversial given that day. After the march, Lewis continued to work in the civil rights movement, and in 1987, he was elected to represent Georgia's 5th District in the U.S. House of Representatives. In January 2009, Lewis sat on the platform at the inauguration of the first African American president, Barack Obama (1961-   ) (see also page 58-59).

3

For those who have said, "Be patient and wait!" we must say, "Patience is a dirty and nasty word." We cannot be patient, we do not want to be free gradually, we want our freedom, and we want it now. We cannot depend on any political party, for the Democrats and the Republicans have betrayed the basic principles of the Declaration of Independence.

John Lewis, 1963

NOW YOU KNOW

- National civil rights leaders organized the Aug. 28, 1963, March on Washington to muster support for the civil rights bill then before Congress.

- Some 200,000 to 250,000 people participated in the event.

- Martin Luther King, Jr., set the tone for the March and inspired many listeners with his "I Have a Dream" speech.

The Johnson Presidency

O N NOV. 22, 1963, PRESIDENT JOHN F. KENNEDY WAS ASSASSINATED in Dallas, Texas, and Vice President Lyndon B. Johnson (1908-1973) became president. Some in the civil rights movement were uneasy about Johnson, a Southerner from Texas. However, President Johnson promptly embraced President Kennedy's civil rights recommendations. Johnson was an expert politician who had long served as Senate majority leader and understood how to work with Congress. Also, the population, shocked and saddened by Kennedy's assassination, was in a mood for bold action. Johnson's administration, from November 1963 to January 1969, oversaw the most sweeping civil rights reforms in the nation's history.

◀ President Lyndon Johnson uses his substantial powers of persuasion to convince Senator Richard Russell (D., Georgia), leader of the Conservative Coalition, to bring around other Southern senators to vote for civil rights legislation before Congress. For decades, Russell had blocked meaningful civil rights legislation that might have protected African Americans from lynching or allowed them to vote.

▶ In his June 4, 1965, speech to the graduating class at Howard University, a historically African American college in Washington, D.C., Lyndon Johnson explains what the civil rights movement in the United States must achieve—equal opportunity for all.

▶ Upon receiving an award from the International Platform Association on Aug. 3, 1965, Johnson reminds his listeners that human freedom remains a radical idea that cannot be taken for granted.

For the task is to give 20 million Negroes the same chance as every other American to learn and grow, to work and share in society, to develop their abilities—physical, mental and spiritual, and to pursue their individual happiness.

Lyndon Johnson, 1965

So, free speech, free press, free religion, the right of free assembly, yes, the right of petition . . . well, they are still radical ideas.

Lyndon Johnson, 1965

3

4

In those tumultuous Great Society years, the president [Johnson] submitted, and Congress enacted, more than 100 major proposals. . . . In those years of do-it-now optimism, presidential speeches were about distributing prosperity more fairly . . . [and] eliminating poverty, hunger, and discrimination in our nation. And when the speeches ended, action followed.

Joseph A. Califano, Jr., 2008

▲ Chief Justice Earl Warren swears in Thurgood Marshall as a justice of the U.S. Supreme Court on Aug. 30, 1967. President Lyndon Johnson (left of Marshall) nominated Marshall to the court, the first African American to serve on the highest court in the land.

◄ At a 2008 celebration of the 100-year anniversary of Johnson's birth, Joseph A. Califano, Jr., (1931-), who served as the president's special assistant, remembers the early years of Johnson's presidency as a time of optimism and action on a wide range of social issues, particularly tackling poverty and fighting racial discrimination.

NOW YOU KNOW

- Vice President Lyndon B. Johnson became president upon John F. Kennedy's assassination on Nov. 22, 1963.
- President Johnson used his legislative experience to persuade Congress to pass a number of civil rights laws and other reforms.
- President Johnson appointed the first African American to the Supreme Court, Thurgood Marshall, in 1967.

The Civil Rights Act of 1964

I**N JUNE 1963, PRESIDENT JOHN F. KENNEDY PROPOSED A CIVIL RIGHTS BILL** that would outlaw racial discrimination in public places. However, the bill met with resistance in Congress. After becoming president in late 1963, Lyndon Johnson worked hard to move the bill through Congress, and on July 2, 1964, he signed the Civil Rights Act of 1964 into law. The law dismantled the long-standing "Jim Crow" system in the South. It outlawed racial discrimination in such public places as hotels, restaurants, and public swimming pools. It also banned job discrimination on the basis of race or sex.

▲ President Lyndon Johnson hands Martin Luther King, Jr., one of the pens Johnson used to sign the Civil Rights Act of 1964. The alliance between the two men—both Southerners, one white and one black—was an odd and uneasy political partnership, but Johnson managed to marshal King's aid to pass major civil rights legislation in a remarkably short span of time.

2

▶ The *preamble* (introduction) to the 1964 Civil Rights Act sets out what the bill was designed to accomplish: guaranteeing African Americans and other minorities the right to vote; and outlawing discrimination in public places, public schools, and in federal programs.

To enforce the constitutional right to vote, to confer *jurisdiction* [the right or power to give out justice] upon the district courts of the United States to provide *injunctive* [the right to issue orders requiring or forbidding a certain action] relief against discrimination in public accommodations, to authorize the Attorney General to *institute* [begin] suits to protect constitutional rights in public *facilities* [places] and public education, to extend the Commission on Civil Rights, to prevent discrimination in federally assisted programs, to establish a Commission on Equal Employment Opportunity, and for other purposes.

from the preamble to the Civil Rights Act, 1964

3

In a dramatically short period of five years, [civil rights activists and protesters] brought change [through] laws like . . . the Civil Rights Act of 1964. . . . This ended state-sanctioned legal political racism in America. Flawed as we are, still burdened by the shadow of slavery, no longer anywhere in this country does the state dictate that any individual is inferior by dint of color.

David Halberstam, 1999

◀ Pulitzer Prize winning history and cultural writer David Halberstam (1934–2007) emphasized the importance of the 1964 Civil Rights Act and its companion 1965 Voting Rights Act in a speech delivered on Oct. 21, 1999, upon accepting the Unitarian Universalist Association's 1999 Melcher Book Award.

NOW YOU KNOW

- President John F. Kennedy proposed a civil rights bill in 1963; President Lyndon Johnson moved the bill through Congress as the Civil Rights Act of 1964.
- The law banned discrimination in public places and job discrimination on the basis of race.
- The law also required programs receiving federal funds to end segregation and racial discrimination, and it authorized the federal government to begin desegregating schools.

The Voting Rights Act

CIVIL RIGHTS ACTIVISTS SOON REALIZED THAT THE 1964 CIVIL RIGHTS ACT did not address an important source of discrimination—the denial of voting rights to African Americans in the South. Since the late 1800's, most Southern states had used poll taxes, literacy tests, and violence to keep African Americans from voting. In March 1965, demonstrators for voting rights were beaten by police in Selma, Alabama. Televised on the nightly news, the violence spurred public backing for a voting rights law. President Johnson and Martin Luther King, Jr., again worked behind the scenes to build political support for the act, which Congress passed in August 1965.

▲ Selma, Alabama, police attack protesters with nightsticks, bullwhips, and tear gas as they cross the Edmund Pettus Bridge on March 7, 1965. About 600 protestors had departed from downtown Selma for a 54-mile (86-kilometer) march to the State Capitol in Montgomery. Protesters wanted to draw attention to the need for federal voting-rights reform. The Selma marchers had to cross the Edmund Pettus Bridge, which was about six blocks away from the starting point of the march. As they emerged from the bridge, police officers sent by Selma's police chief attacked. More than 50 of the marchers sustained injuries in what came to be known as "Bloody Sunday." Television coverage of the attack shocked the nation.

2

Southern state	Votes cast in 1960 presidential election	Total population	Northern/ Western state	Votes cast in 1960 presidential election	Total population
Arkansas	429,000	1,788,000	Oregon	776,000	1,773,000
Mississippi	298,000	2,180,000	Kansas	929,000	2,178,000
Virginia	771,000	3,978,000	Wisconsin	1,729,000	3,964,000

▲ A comparison between states in the South and the North with similar populations reveals a huge difference in the number of people who turned out to vote in the 1960 presidential election. The differences were mainly due to Jim Crow laws that were designed to bar African Americans from voting. These included intimidation outside polling places; poll taxes, that is, a tax imposed upon the right to vote, which many African Americans could not afford; and literacy tests, which uneducated blacks were unable to pass. Uneducated whites were "grandfathered" in, that is, if they voted in the past, they were allowed to continue to do so.

▶ The Voting Rights Act became law on Aug. 6, 1965. It banned literacy tests and poll taxes. In places where the vote had been unjustly denied, the law provided for federal officials to supervise voter registration and forbid major changes in voting laws without the approval of the attorney general. It gave the vote to hundreds of thousands of Southern blacks who had never voted before.

3

No voting qualification or *prerequisite* [something required beforehand] to voting, or standard, practice, or procedure shall be imposed or applied by any State or political subdivision to deny or *abridge* [restrict] the right of any citizen of the United States to vote on account of race or color.

from Section 2 of the Voting Rights Act, 1965

NOW YOU KNOW

- Since the late 1800's, many blacks in the South had been prevented from voting in elections.

- On March 7, 1965, police in Selma, Alabama, beat demonstrators on a march for the right to vote. The violence, telecast on the nightly news, shocked the nation.

- Congress passed an effective reform, the Voting Rights Act, which allowed hundreds of thousands of African Americans in the South the vote for the first time.

New Voices

MARTIN LUTHER KING, JR., SPOKE IN FAVOR OF NONVIOLENCE, but some prominent African Americans spoke in more *militant* (aggressive) terms in the mid-1960's. Many younger African Americans became disappointed with the pace of the civil rights movement, and some turned away from King's and Gandhi's principles to adopt more violent tactics. Malcolm X (1925-1965), a leader of the Nation of Islam (sometimes called the "Black Muslims"), warned white America of God's anger if *amends* (something given or paid to make up for a wrong or injury done) were not made for centuries of slavery and racism.

◀ Malcolm X in a photo taken shortly before his assassination by three gunmen in New York City on Feb. 21, 1965. Although Malcolm X had frequently spoken of whites in harsh terms, he began to rethink his position on integration and other issues of race after breaking with the Nation of Islam in 1964.

So we of this present generation are also witnessing how the enslavement of millions of Black people in this country is now bringing White America to her hour of judgment, to her downfall as a respected nation. And even those Americans who are blinded by childlike patriotism can see that it is only a matter of time before White America too will be utterly destroyed by her own sins, and all traces of her former glory will be removed from this planet forever.

Malcolm X, 1963

▶ In his 1963 speech "God's Judgment of White America," Malcolm X preaches that God's wrath will come down on white America for the sins of slavery and racism. The Nation of Islam leader was born Malcolm Little, but he rejected his inherited last name as the name of slaves. "X" was intended to represent his lost African name. When Malcolm X broke with the Nation of Islam to become a Sunni Muslim, he again changed his name, to El-Hajj Malik El-Shabazz.

▶ Civil rights activist Stokely Carmichael (1941-1998) makes the sign of Black Power, a raised fist. He rose to prominence first as a leader of the Student Nonviolent Coordinating Committee and had taken part in the 1961 Freedom Rides and many other civil rights actions. As a result of this activism, Carmichael was subjected to many arrests and beatings. In 1966, he helped form a political party of African Americans in Alabama that adopted the symbol of the black panther. The party and its symbol was the inspiration for the Black Panther Party founded in California by Bobby Seale (1936-   ) and Huey P. Newton (1942-1989), also in 1966.

The only time I hear people talk about nonviolence is when black people move to defend themselves against white people. Black people cut themselves every night in the ghetto—nobody talks about nonviolence. Lyndon Baines Johnson is busy bombing . . . Vietnam—nobody talks about nonviolence. White people beat up black people every day—nobody talks about nonviolence. But as soon as black people start to move, the double standard comes into being.

Stokely Carmichael, 1966

◀ Stokely Carmichael may have coined the term "black power" in his "Black Power" speech given in October 1966 in Berkeley, California. Carmichael came to be regarded as the "honorary prime minister" of the Black Panther Party. He eventually left the United States for Africa, where he died.

NOW YOU KNOW

- Some African Americans turned away from Martin Luther King's philosophy of nonviolence.

- Malcolm X, a strong, new voice in the civil rights movement was assassinated in 1965.

- The Black Panther Party, created in 1966, promoted black pride and black power. Members included the founders, Bobby Seale and Huey Newton, and former SNCC leader Stokely Carmichael. The party's violent conflicts with the police were one cause of its eventual decline.

Black Ghettos and Urban Riots

UNHAPPINESS AND FRUSTRATION AMONG AFRICANS AMERICANS living in big-city slums boiled over into riots during the summers of 1964, 1965, 1966, and 1967. The Great Migration had brought many thousands of African Americans, filled with high hopes for a better life, to big Northern cities from the rural South. Some of the migrants had prospered and improved their lives. However, with no experience of city life and little or no education—as well as white-on-black prejudice—many others found it difficult to do well. As a result, slums populated by African Americans developed in many American cities. During the 1960's, the term *ghetto* (any segregated area of a city) was often used to describe these slums.

▲ An angry crowd confronts National Guardsmen during a riot in Newark, New Jersey, in 1967. Six days of rioting and looting in Newark in July of that year left 26 dead, hundreds injured, and parts of the city in ruins. Anger and frustration at discrimination and lack of economic opportunity exploded into riots in a number of large U.S. cities in the mid-1960's, including Philadelphia (1964), Los Angeles (1965), Chicago (1966). and Detroit (1967).

②

"Burn, baby, burn!"
Nathaniel Montague

◀ Disk jockey Nathaniel "Magnificent" Montague (1928-) used the phrase "Burn, baby, burn!" while playing *R & B* (rhythm & blues) music on KGFJ, a Los Angeles radio station. The phrase was picked up and chanted by rioters in the Watts neighborhood of Los Angeles in 1965 as they set fire to stores. It became a national catch phrase of the era.

▶ After the Newark and Detroit riots in 1967, President Lyndon B. Johnson appointed the National Advisory Commission on Civil Disorders to investigate the causes of urban race riots and submit a report to him. The commission submitted its report—informally called "the Kerner Report" in honor of the commission chair, Otto Kerner, Jr. (1908-1976), the governor of Illinois—to the president in 1968. The report emphasized the frustration and lack of opportunity experienced by many ghetto residents as a primary cause of urban race riots.

③

Violence cannot build a better society. Disruption and disorder nourish *repression* [keeping down or putting down a people or group], not justice. They strike at the freedom of every citizen. . . . Segregation and poverty have created in the racial ghetto a destructive environment totally unknown to most white Americans. . . . What white Americans have never fully understood—but what the Negro can never forget—is that white society is deeply implicated in the ghetto. White institutions created it, white institutions maintain it, and white society *condones* [excuses] it. . . . It is time to make good the promises of American democracy to all citizens—urban and rural, white and black, Spanish-surnames, American Indian, and every minority group.

from the "Report of the National Advisory Commission on Civil Disorders," 1968

NOW YOU KNOW

- Devastating riots broke out in the African American communities of many large U.S. cities in the mid-1960's.

- Some of the worst riots—with loss of life and property—occurred in the Watts neighborhood of Los Angeles, in Newark, and in Detroit.

- In its 1968 report to the president, the Commission on Civil Disorders said that the anger and frustration of African Americans trapped in ghettos was the chief cause of the riots.

The Death of King

On April 4, 1968, Martin Luther King, Jr., was shot and killed in Memphis, Tennessee. Within hours, riots broke out in at least 100 African American communities across the country. King's murder helped President Lyndon Johnson persuade Congress to pass the Civil Rights Act of 1968. This law, also known as the Fair Housing Act, prohibited racial discrimination in the sale and rental of housing. In 1983, Congress set aside the third Monday in January—the Monday nearest King's birthday, January 15—as Martin Luther King, Jr., Day, a federal holiday.

1

Like anybody, I would like to live a long life. Longevity has its place. But I'm not concerned about that now. I just want to do God's will. And He's allowed me to go up to the mountain. And I've looked over. And I've seen the promised land. I may not get there with you. But I want you to know tonight, that we, as a people, will get to the promised land!

Martin Luther King, Jr., April 3, 1968

◀ The mountaintop Martin Luther King, Jr., refers to in his "I've Been to the Mountaintop" speech is from the Old Testament of the Bible, in which God takes Moses, the leader of his people, to a mountaintop and shows him the land promised to his people, the Israelites. Moses leads his people out of slavery, but does not himself live to enter the Promised Land. King gave the speech in Memphis, Tennessee, on the day before he was assassinated.

▶ Aids to Martin Luther King, Jr., point to a window from which an assassin shot the civil rights leader, whose body lies on the balcony of the Lorraine Motel in Memphis on the night of April 4, 1968. The assassin, James Earl Ray (1928-1998), was subsequently captured, tried, and convicted for the crime. He spent the rest of his life in prison. However, Ray later claimed that he had not acted alone and had not fired the weapon. The controversy has never been solved. Today, the Lorraine Motel houses the National Civil Rights Museum.

2

3

▲ Fire engulfs a neighborhood on Chicago's West Side in April 1968 during riots following the murder of Martin Luther King, Jr. The assassination triggered shock, grief, and anger, which erupted in violence in black neighborhoods across the United States. In Chicago, looters and arsonists set more than 125 fires that consumed all or parts of 28 blocks. Eleven people—all African American—were killed, more than 500 others were injured, and 1,000 people were left homeless. It took decades for the scars to heal in Chicago and in inner cities throughout the country.

▶ In King's 1967 book, *Where Do We Go From Here? Chaos or Community?*, he states his belief that only nonviolent solutions have a hope of solving the world's problems.

4

The ultimate weakness of violence is that it is a descending spiral, *begetting* [creating] the very thing it seeks to destroy. Instead of *diminishing* [lessening] evil, it multiplies it. . . . So it goes.

Martin Luther King, Jr., 1967

NOW YOU KNOW

- Martin Luther King, Jr., was shot and killed in Memphis, Tennessee, on April 4, 1968.

- In the wake of King's assassination, violence broke out in African American communities across the nation.

- The King assassination and its aftermath prompted Congress to pass the 1968 Civil Rights Act, which prohibited discrimination in the selling or renting of housing.

Affirmative Action

BETWEEN 1970 AND THE EARLY 1990'S, THE NUMBER OF AFRICAN AMERICANS enrolled in colleges rose from approximately 600,000 to 1.3 million. This increase was partly the result of affirmative-action programs adopted by predominantly white colleges and universities. Affirmative-action programs attempt to increase the numbers of women and minorities in education, business, and other areas. Many businesses also began affirmative-action programs in the 1970's. Affirmative action has been a controversial policy. Some people believe affirmative action is necessary to help groups who have been discriminated against in the past to catch up with the rest of society. Others believe that affirmative action unfairly affects the right of individuals to be treated according to their abilities. Another remedy—busing—was designed to improve educational opportunities for minorities in U.S. public schools. In the 1960's, some U.S. cities tried to integrate their school systems by busing students from schools in their own neighborhoods to schools in other neighborhoods.

◀ Police escort school buses in Boston, Massachusetts, in September 1974. Beginning in the late 1960's, many students were bused from their neighborhood schools to other schools to satisfy court-ordered desegregation rulings. The practice encountered much resistance from the public, particularly from parents with school-age children. In response to busing and urban unrest, many white residents of cities moved to the suburbs, and large cities became even more segregated.

▶ A 1972 *Time* magazine article records the anger and resistance stirred in the United States to integration efforts that used busing children to schools outside their own neighborhoods. In the 1990's, the Supreme Court placed limits on how much busing school systems were obligated to carry out to achieve integration. Today, many black students continue to attend segregated schools.

2

For years, busing was primarily a Southern concern as courts ordered school districts to *dismantle* [take apart] dual school systems. But in the past year, court-dictated busing spread to Northern cities, giving rise to boycotts and *sporadic* [occasional] violence in such *disparate* [different] places as Pontiac, Michigan, and San Francisco's Chinatown. One reaction to the uproar was a proposed constitutional amendment prohibiting busing. . . . A recent Gallup poll showed that 77 percent of Americans—black and white—disapproved of busing as a means of racially balancing school enrollment.

Time, Feb. 28, 1972

3

With my academic achievement in high school, I was accepted rather readily at Princeton [a university in New Jersey] and equally as fast at Yale [a university in Connecticut], but my test scores were not comparable to that of my classmates. And that's been shown by statistics, there are reasons for that. There are cultural biases [questions that a person of one culture would find easier to answer than a person of another culture] built into testing, and that was one of the motivations for the concept of affirmative action to try to balance out those effects.

Sonia Sotomayor, early 1990's

◀ In a panel discussion, then U.S. District Court Judge Sonia Sotomayor (1954-) describes her experiences with affirmative action. In 2009, Sotomayor became the first Hispanic justice on the U.S. Supreme Court. From a poor family in the New York City borough of the Bronx, and of Puerto Rican descent, Sotomayor states she would not likely have been admitted to an important school like Princeton on her test scores alone. Nevertheless, Sotomayor worked hard and graduated from Princeton with highest honors. She then attended Yale Law School.

NOW YOU KNOW

- Affirmative-action policies were designed to increase minority and female representation in schools, businesses, and other areas.

- Some believe that affirmative action prevents people from being judged on their own abilities.

- The policy of busing for desegregation was designed to achieve desired racial mixes in the public school systems of cities and counties.

New Black Leaders

AFTER THE PASSAGE OF THE VOTING RIGHTS ACT OF 1965, many African American leaders stressed the use of political means to solve problems affecting black communities. They urged more African Americans to vote and to run for office. Soon, blacks were being elected to high offices across the country. In 1973, Tom Bradley (1917-1998) was elected the first African American mayor of Los Angeles; and in 1974, Maynard H. Jackson (1938-2003) was elected the first black mayor of Atlanta; and Coleman Young (1918-1997) was elected the first black mayor of Detroit, also in 1974. In 1983, Harold Washington (1922-1987) was elected as the first African American mayor of Chicago; and in 1989, David N. Dinkins (1927-) won election as the first black mayor of New York City. The first African American to be elected governor of a state was L. Douglas Wilder (1931-), elected in Virginia in 1990. African Americans also served increasingly in such high-level appointed offices as secretary of the U.S. Department of State.

▶ Colin Powell (1937-) was the first African American to serve as secretary of state. He joined the army in 1958, became a general in 1989, and ended his service career as chairman of the Joint Chiefs of Staff, the highest U.S. military advisory group to the president. Condoleezza Rice (1954-) followed Powell in the position of secretary of state. She became the first African American woman to serve in the post.

2

. . . in one role I want government to be vigorous and active, and that is in ensuring the protections of the Constitution to all Americans. Our Constitution and our national conscience demand that every American be accorded dignity and respect, receive the same treatment under the law, and enjoy equal opportunity. The hard-won civil-rights legislation of the 1960's, which I benefited from, was fought for by presently derided liberals, courageous leaders who won these gains over the opposition of those hiding behind transparent arguments of "states rights" and "property rights."

Colin Powell, 1996

▶ In 1998, *Time* magazine published a *eulogy* [praise of a deceased person] for Tom Bradley that was written by Willie Lewis Brown, Jr., (1934-   ), then mayor of San Francisco. Bradley had been mayor of Los Angeles from 1973 to 1993. He joined the L.A. Police Department in 1940, eventually becoming the department's first African American lieutenant. He entered politics in the 1960's and has been the only African American to serve as mayor of Los Angeles.

◀ In his 1996 book *My American Journey*, Colin Powell, who was born in New York City to Jamaican immigrants, writes about his gratitude to those who fought for civil rights legislation in the 1960's. His statement—"the opposition of those hiding behind transparent arguments of 'states rights' "—refers to the argument that civil rights legislation was unconstitutional. For years, segregationist legislators claimed that such laws would violate the 10th Amendment to the U.S. Constitution. This amendment reads, "The powers not delegated to the United States by the Constitution, nor prohibited by it to the States, are reserved to the States respectively, or to the people."

3

As mayor of Los Angeles, Tom Bradley was a healer of social divisions and a visionary who shepherded the transformation of an unruly town into a great city. The grandson of slaves, the son of Texas sharecroppers, he broke through racial barriers because there was simply no surrender in him.

Time, Oct. 12, 1998

NOW YOU KNOW

- As a result of civil rights activism and the Voting Rights Act of 1965, many African Americans became politically active and began to vote regularly in elections.

- With greater numbers of African Americans voting, greater numbers of African Americans were elected to city, state, and national offices in the 1970's and afterward.

- In the years that followed, African Americans increasingly held high offices. Colin Powell served as chairman of the Joint Chiefs of Staff (1989-1993) and as secretary of state (2001-2005); Condoleezza Rice served as secretary of state from 2005 to 2009.

President Barack Obama

On Nov. 4, 2008, Barack Obama became the first African American to be elected president of the United States. Obama had enjoyed a rapid political rise. From 1995 to 2004, he was a member of the Illinois Senate. In July 2004, he gained national attention by giving the *keynote address* (the speech that presents the main themes or ideas for a meeting or convention) at the Democratic Party's national convention in Boston. In November 2004, Obama (D., Illinois) was elected to the U.S. Senate. He served in the Senate from early 2005 to early 2009, when he became president. To many Americans, the election of an African American as president symbolized the fall of the final barrier to full political participation by African Americans.

◀ Barack Obama delivering the keynote address to the 2004 Democratic Party Convention in Boston, July 27, 2004

▶ In his keynote speech at the Democratic National Convention in 2004, Barack Obama, then an Illinois state senator, revealed his diverse heritage: his father was an African from Kenya, and his mother was born to a white family from Kansas.

Tonight is a particular honor for me because, let's face it, my presence on this stage is pretty unlikely. My father was a foreign student, born and raised in a small village in Kenya. He grew up herding goats, went to school in a tin-roof shack. His father—my grandfather—was a cook, a domestic servant to the British.

But my grandfather had larger dreams for his son. Through hard work and perseverance my father got a scholarship to study in a magical place, America, that shone as a beacon of freedom and opportunity to so many who had come before.

While studying here, my father met my mother. . . . Her father worked on oil rigs and farms through most of the Depression. The day after Pearl Harbor my grandfather signed up for duty . . . my grandmother raised their baby and went to work on a bomber assembly line. . . . And they, too, had big dreams for their daughter. A common dream, born of two continents.

Barack Obama, July 27, 2004

3

I never imagined, I never even had any idea I would live to see an African American president of the United States. . . . We have witnessed tonight in America a revolution of values, a revolution of ideals. There's been a transformation of America, and it will have unbelievable influence on the world.

John Lewis, 2008

◀ On the night of Obama's election, U.S. Representative John Lewis (D., Georgia), a hero of the Civil Rights Movement, expressed joy at the election of a fellow African American to the presidency. He saw Obama's election as a transformative moment not only of the United States, but also for the world.

▼ Barack Obama takes the oath of office as 44th president of the United States on Jan. 20, 2009. Beside him are his wife, Michelle (1964-), and daughters Malia (1998-) and Sasha (2001-).

4

NOW YOU KNOW

- On Nov. 4, 2008, Barack Obama became the first African American to be elected president of the United States.

- His father was born and raised in Kenya; his mother was born into a white family from Kansas.

- For many African Americans, the election of Barack Obama marked the beginning of a new era in U.S. politics.

Timeline

1776	The Declaration of Independence is adopted on July 4.
1787	The U.S. Constitution is written.
1857	The U.S. Supreme Court in *Dred Scott v. Sandford* determines that no black person—either free or slave—can claim U.S. citizenship.
1861	The American Civil War begins on April 12 at Fort Sumter, South Carolina.
1863	President Abraham Lincoln issues the Emancipation Proclamation.
1865	The Confederacy surrenders at Appomattox Court House in Virginia to end the Civil War. (Note, some soldiers did not hear of the surrender, so battles continue into May.)
1865	The period of Reconstruction begins.
1865	The 13th Amendment to the Constitution, which prohibits slavery in the United States, is ratified on December 6.
1868	The 14th Amendment to the Constitution, which grants citizenship to anyone born in the United States, is ratified on July 9.
1870's	Southern states begin to enact Jim Crow laws.
1896	The U.S. Supreme Court in *Plessy v. Ferguson* decides that "separate but equal" facilities for blacks and whites are acceptable in railroad cars.
1909	NAACP is organized.
around 1914	The Great Migration begins.
1933	President Franklin Delano Roosevelt begins his New Deal economic program to help end the Great Depression and give assistance to Americans of all races.
1948	Segregation is outlawed in the U.S. armed forces.
1954	The *Brown v. Board of Education of Topeka* ruling by the Supreme Court strikes down the concept of "separate but equal" being acceptable or fair in public schools.
1955	Rosa Parks refuses to give up her seat in the white section of a segregated bus in Montgomery, Alabama, on December 1.
1957	When African American students enroll in Little Rock Central High School, rioting erupts. Federal troops escort black students into the school.
1961	Freedom riders—both African American and white volunteers—integrate buses across states in the South. Violence against the riders is extreme.
1963	Peaceful protestors for civil rights in Birmingham, Alabama, are attacked by police with dogs and water hoses while demonstrating in April and May.
1963	Martin Luther King, Jr., and other civil rights activists lead the March on Washington on August 28.
1963	President John F. Kennedy is assassinated in Dallas, Texas, on November 22 and Lyndon B. Johnson becomes president.
1963	Martin Luther King, Jr., writes the "Letter from Birmingham Jail" on April 16.
1964	Civil Rights Act signed into law on July 2. The act bans discrimination because of a person's color, race, national origin, religion, or sex.
1965	Malcolm X is assassinated in New York City on February 21.
1965	Protestors at a peaceful march in Selma, Alabama, on March 7 are attacked by police.
1965	The Voting Rights Act is signed into law on August 6. The act makes voting laws that discriminated against black voters illegal.
1968	Martin Luther King, Jr., is assassinated on April 4 in Memphis, Tennessee.
1970's	Busing of students to achieve integration of schools becomes more common.
1970's-2000's	African Americans gain higher elected offices and achieve higher enrollment numbers at colleges and universities.
2008	Barack Obama is elected president.

Sources

4–5 Document 2 – United States. The Declaration of Independence. 1776. *Project Gutenberg*. Web. 14 May 2010. Document 3 – National Assembly of France. Declaration of the Rights of Man and of the Citizen. 1789. *The Avalon Project*. Web. 14 May 2010.

6–7 Document 1 – United States. The Constitution of the United States. Art. 4, Sec. 2, Cl. 3. 1787. *Project Gutenberg*. Web. 14 May 2010 Document 2 – United States. Supreme Court. *The Case of Dred Scott in the United States Supreme Court. The Full Opinions of Chief Justice Taney and Justice Curtis...* New York: The Tribune Association, 1860. *Internet Archive*. Web. 14 May 2010.

8–9 Document 2 – Douglass, Frederick. *The Life and Times of Frederick Douglass*. Hartford: Park, 1882. *Internet Archive*. Web. 14 May 2010. Document 3 – United States. Constitution of the United States. Amendment 13. Ratified on 6 Dec. 1865. *The Avalon Project*. Web. 14 May 2010.

10–11 Document 2 – United States. The Constitution of the United States. Amendment 14, Sec. 1. Ratified on 9 July 1868. www.ourdocuments.gov. Web. 14 May 2010. Document 3 – Whitman, Walt. "Respondez!" *Leaves of Grass*. 1872. *The Walt Whitman Archive*. Web. 14 May 2010.

12–13 Douglass, Frederick. "Reconstruction." *Atlantic Monthly* Dec. 1866: 761-5. *Google Books*. Web. 14 May 2010. Document 3 – Greeley, Horace, ed. *The Tribune Almanac and Political Register for 1869*. New York: The Tribune Association, 1869. *Google Books*. Web. 14 May 2010.

14–15 Document 1 – Randall, Vernellia R., ed. "Examples of Jim Crow Laws." *Race, Racism and the Law*. Vernellia R. Randall, 2001. Web. 14 May 2010. Document 2 – Constitution of the State of Louisiana. 1898. In Thorpe, Francis N., comp. *The Federal and State Constitutions ....*Vol. 3. Washington: GPO, 1909. *Google Books*. Web. 14 May 2010.

16–17 Document 2 – Washington, Booker T. *The Booker T. Washington Papers. Volume 3, 1889-95*. University of Illinois Press, 1974. Print. Document 4 – Du Bois, W.E.B. "Address to the Country." Aug. 1906. In *W.E.B. Du Bois: A Reader*. New York: H. Holt, 1995. Print.

18–19 Document 2 – Allan, Lewis. "Strange Fruit." 1937. Available in *Encyclopedia of American Race Riots*. Westport, CT: Greenwood, 2007. Print. Document 4 – Wells-Barnett, Ida B. "Lynch Law in America." *Arena* 23.1 (1900): 15-24. *Google Books*. Web. 14 May 2010.

20–21 Document 1 – Locke, Alain. "Harlem." *Survey Graphic* 6.6 (1925): 29-30. *Google Books*. Web. 14 May 2010. Document 3 – Scott, Emmett J., comp. "Additional Letters of Negro Migrants of 1916-1918." *Journal of Negro History* 4.4 (1919): 413-65. *Google Books*. Web. 14 May 2010.

22–23 Document 1 – "Race Riots and Murders in Atlanta." *Independent* [New York] 27 Sept. 1906: 713-14. *Google Books*. Web. 14 May 2010. Document 3 – Garrison, Oswald Villard. "The Call." 12 Feb. 1909. *African American Odyssey: The Booker T. Washington Era*. Web. 14 May 2010.

24–25 Document 2 – Torricelli, Robert G., and Andrew Carroll, eds. *In Our Own Words* New York: Kodansha, 1999. Print. Document 4 – Foner, Philip S., and Ronald L. Lewis, eds. *The Era of Post-War Prosperity and the Great Depression, 1920-1936*. Temple University Press, 1981. Print.

26–27 Document 1 – Cockfield, Jamie H. "All Blood Runs Red." *Legacy: A Supplement to American Heritage* Feb./Mar. 1995: 7-15. PDF file. Document 4 – Truman, Harry S. Executive Order 9981. 26 July 1948. *Harry S. Truman Library and Museum*. Web. 14 May 2010.

28–29 Document 3 – Brown v. Board of Education of Topeka. 347 US 483. Supreme Court of the US. 1954. Available in *Documents of American History: Volume II, Since 1898*. Ed. Henry S. Commager. 10th ed. Englewood Cliffs, NJ: Prentice Hall, 1988. Print.

30–31 Document 2 –Parks, Rosa and Haskins, Jim. *Rosa Parks: My Story*. Dial Books, 1992. Print. Document 4 – Parks, Rosa. Quoted in "Rosa Parks, Matriarch of Civil Rights, Dies at 92." *MSNBC.com*, 25 Oct. 2005. Web. 14 May 2010.

32–33 Document 2 – Gandhi, Mohandas. *Non-violent resistance (Satyagraha)*. New York: Schocken Books, 1961. Print. Document 4 – King,

Martin Luther, Jr., Nobel Peace Prize acceptance speech. 10 Dec. 1964. *Nobelprize.org*. Web. 13 May 2010.

34–35 Document 2 – Knox, Joe. "An Old Lesson Relearned." News & Record [Greensboro, NC] 1 Feb 1970: n. pag. *AllBusiness.com*. Web. 13 May 2010. Document 3 – Farmer, James. Quoted in Severo, Richard. "James Farmer, Civil Rights Giant in the 50's and 60's, Is Dead at 79." *New York Times*, 10 July 1999. Web. 13 May 2010.

36–37 Document 2 – King, Martin Luther, Jr., "Letter from Birmingham City Jail." 16 Apr. 1963. In *A Testament of Hope: The Essential Writings and Speeches of Martin Luther King, Jr.* Ed. James M. Washington. San Francisco: HarperCollins, 1991. Print. Document 4 – Kennedy, John F. "Civil Rights Message." 11 June 1963. In *Ebony* Sept. 1963: 233-4. *Google Books*. Web. 13 May 2010.

38–39 Document 1 – Sitton, Claude. "Birmingham Bomb Kills 4 Negro Girls in Church." *New York Times* 16 Sept. 1963: 1. *New York Times: On This Day*. Web. 13 May 2010. Document 3 – "4 August 1964: Three Civil Rights Activists Found Dead." *BBC On This Day, 1950-2005*. BBC, n.d. Web. 13 May 2010.

40–41 Document 2 – King, Martin Luther, Jr., "I Have a Dream." 28 Aug. 1963. *MLK Online*. Web. 13 May 2010. Document 3 – Lewis, John. Speech at the March on Washington. 28 Aug. 1963. In Lewis, John, and Michael D'Orso. *Walking with the Wind*. Simon & Schuster, 1998. Print.

42–43 Document 2 – Johnson, Lyndon B. Commencement Address at Howard University (4 June 1965) and Remarks to the International Platform Association (3 Aug. 1965). *American Presidency Project*. Web. 13 May 2010. Document 4 – Califano, Joseph A., Jr. "Seeing Is Believing: The Enduring Legacy of Lyndon Johnson." Keynote Address at the Lyndon B. Johnson Centennial Celebration. Kaiser Family Foundation, Washington, D.C. 19 May 2008. PDF file.

44–45 Document 2 – Civil Rights Act of 1964. 2 July 1964. *www .ourdocuments.gov*. Web. 13 May 2010. Document 3 – Halberstam, David. Melcher Book Award speech. 21 Oct. 1999. In "David Halberstam Accepts 1999 Melcher Prize" *UUH.org*. Unitarian Universalists Association of Congregations, n.d. Web. 13 May 2010.

46–47 Document 3 – Voting Rights Act of 1965. 6 Aug. 1965. *The Avalon Project*. Web. 13 May 2010.

48–49 Document 2 – Malcolm X. "God's Judgment of White America." Speech in New York 4 Dec. 1963. In *The End of White World Supremacy*. New York: Arcade, 1971. Print. Document 4 – Carmichael, Stokely. "Black Power." Speech in Berkley, CA, 29 Oct. 1966. In *Stokely Speaks*. New York: Random House, 1971. Print.

50–51 Document 2 – Montague, Nathaniel. *Burn, Baby! Burn! The Autobiography of Magnificent Montague*. University of Illinois Press, 2003. Print. Document 3 – United States. Kerner Commission. *Report on the National Advisory Commission on Civil Disorders*. New York: Bantam Books, 1968. Print.

52–53 Document 1 – King, Martin Luther, Jr., "I See the Promised Land." 3 Apr. 1963. *MLK Online*. Web. 13 May 2010. Document 4 – King, Martin Luther, Jr., *Where Do We Go from Here: Chaos or Community?* New York: Harper & Row, 1967. Print.

54–55 Document 2 – "The Busing Issue Boils Over." *Time* 28 Feb. 1972: 14-15. Print. Document 3 – Sotomayor, Sonia. Comments on a videotape dated early 1990's. Quoted in Savage, Charlie. "Videos Shed New Light on Sotomayor's Positions." *New York Times* 10 June 2009. Web. 13 May 2010.

56–57 Document 2 – Powell, Colin. *My American Journey*. New York: Ballantine Books, 1996. Print. Document 3 – Brown, Willie Lewis, Jr. "Eulogy." *Time* 12 Oct. 1998: 29. Print.

58–59 Document 2 – Obama, Barack. Keynote speech to the Democratic National Convention. 27 July 2004. Available in *Dreams from My Father*. New York : Three Rivers Press, 2004. Print. Document 3 – Lewis, John. 2008 . Quoted in "African-Americans Savor a Historic Moment." *MSNBC.com*, 5 Nov. 2008. Web. 14 May 2010.

Additional resources

Books

The Bill of Rights (True Book series), by Christine Taylor-Butler, Children's Press, 2008

The Civil Rights Movement: An Interactive History Adventure (You Choose Books series), by Heather Adamson, Capstone Press, 2009

A Dream of Freedom: The Civil Rights Movement from 1954 to 1968, by Diane McWhorter, Scholastic, 2004

Extraordinary People of the Civil Rights Movement (Extraordinary People series), by Sheila Jackson Hardy and P. Stephen Hardy, Children's Press, 2007

A Look at the Thirteenth and Fourteenth Amendments: Slavery Abolished, Equal Protection Established (The Constitution of the United States series), by John R. Conway, MyReportLinks.com Books, 2008

M.L.K.: Journey of a King, by Tonya Bolden and Bob Adelman, Abrams Books for Young Readers, 2007

Separate but Equal: The Desegregation of America's Schools (Lucent Library of Black History series), Lucent Books, 2007

Websites

http://chnm.gmu.edu/courses/122/recon/chron.html
"A Timeline of Reconstruction" contains links to more detailed coverage of people, organizations, and legislation of the period, from 1865 to 1877.

http://memory.loc.gov/ammem/aaohtml/exhibit/aointro.html
This website for the U.S. Library of Congress exhibition "The African American Odyssey: A Quest for Full Citizenship" contains background information about the documents and artifacts on display.

http://www.ontheissues.org/2008/Barack_Obama_Civil_Rights.htm
A collection of quotations from various speeches by Barack Obama, in which he addresses civil rights issues.

http://teacher.scholastic.com/rosa/index.htm
All about Rosa Parks and how she influenced the civil rights movement.

http://www.voicesofcivilrights.org/voices.html
"Voices of Civil Rights" features personal stories told by people who experienced the events of the civil rights movement.

Index

Index

Acknowledgements

AKG-Images: 6, 9, (North Wind Picture Archives), 8; **American-Rails.com:** 21 (Resource guide to American railroading); **Art Archives:** 22 (Domenica del Corriere/Gianni Dagli Orti); **Bridgeman Art Library:** 10, 13, 7, 16, (Peter Newark American Pictures); **Corbis:** 4 (© Rick Friedman), 5, 24, 28. 34, 39, 43, 44, 50, (© Bettmann), 56 (© Brooks Kraft), 59 (© Ralf-finn Hestoft), 26; **CSU Archives:** 28 (Everett Collection/Rex Features); **Culver Pictures:** 17, (The Art Archives); **Getty:** 27, 49, 33, 40, 48, 52, 53 (Time Life Pictures), 58 (AFP); **Lyndon B. Johnson Library and Museum:** 42; **Mary Evans Picture Library:** 23; **NAACP Collection:** 20; **Smithsonian Institution:** 15 (Division of Politics and Reform, National Museum of American History); **Topfoto:** 18, 37, 46, 12, 19, 20, 29, 36, (AP), 30, 31, 32, (The Granger Collection), 25, 35, (Topham Picturepoint).

Cover main image: **Corbis** (Brooks Kraft); inset image: **Topfoto** (AP)